Please

By Janine Amos   Illustrated by Annabel Spenceley

Gareth Stevens Publishing
A WORLD ALMANAC EDUCATION GROUP COMPANY

Please visit our web site at: www.garethstevens.com
For a free color catalog describing Gareth Stevens'
list of high-quality books and multimedia programs,
call 1-800-542-2595 (USA) or 1-800-461-9120 (Canada).
Gareth Stevens Publishing's Fax: (414) 332-3567.

Library of Congress Cataloging-in-Publication Data

Amos, Janine.
    Please / by Janine Amos; illustrated by Annabel Spenceley.
        p. cm. — (Courteous kids)
    Includes bibliographical references.
    ISBN 0-8368-2806-2 (lib. bdg.)
    1. Courtesy—Juvenile literature. 2. Children—Conduct of
life. [1. Etiquette. 2. Conduct of life.] I. Spenceley, Annabel, ill.
II. Title.
BJ1533.C9A466   2001
395.1'22—dc21   00-049296

This edition first published in 2001 by
Gareth Stevens Publishing
A World Almanac Education Group Company
330 West Olive Street, Suite 100
Milwaukee, WI 53212 USA

Gareth Stevens editor: Anne Miller
Cover design: Joel Bucaro

This edition © 2001 by Gareth Stevens, Inc. First published by Cherrytree Press,
a subsidiary of Evans Brothers Limited. © 1999 by Cherrytree (a member of the
Evans Group of Publishers), 2A Portman Mansions, Chiltern Street, London
W1M 1LE, United Kingdom. This U.S. edition published under license from
Evans Brothers Limited. Additional end matter © 2001 by Gareth Stevens, Inc.

Printed in the United States of America

1 2 3 4 5 6 7 8 9 05 04 03 02

Ben's Ball

Ali and Ben are playing.
Ali kicks the ball hard.

4

The ball goes over the bushes and
lands in Mr. Ashley's garden.

Ali asks for the ball.

Mr. Ashley throws the ball back.

The next time the ball lands in
Mr. Ashley's garden, Ben asks for it.

Why does Mr. Ashley say no?

How does Ben feel?

How does Mr. Ashley feel?

Ben asks again.

How does Mr. Ashley feel now?

Mr. Ashley hands the ball back to Ben.

Kate's Juice

Kate can't reach the juice.
She tells Jack to get it.

Jack won't.

Why won't Jack help Kate?
How does he feel?

18

Kate thinks about it.
What could she do?

She asks Jack for help and says "please."

Monica's Story

Monica wants Mom to read to her.

Mom is tired.

Monica says, "Please."
Mom thinks about it.

How does Monica feel?
How does Mom feel?

Monica looks at her book while she waits.

Mom drinks her tea.

Then Mom reads Monica a story.

How do Monica and Mom feel now?

More Books to Read

Barney Says, "Please and Thank You." Stephen White (Lyrick Studios)

Just Say Please. Gina Mayer (Golden Books)

Manners. Aliki (Greenwillow)

Pass the Peas, Please: A Book of Manners. Dina Anastasio (Roxbury Park)

Note to Parents and Teachers

The questions that appear in **boldface** type can be used to initiate discussion with your children or class. Encourage them to think of possible answers before continuing with the story.

Additional Resources

Parents and teachers may find these materials useful in discussing manners with children:

Video: *Manners Can Be Fun!* (ETI-KIDS, Ltd.) This video includes a teacher's guide.

Web Site: *Preschoolers Today: Where Have the Manners Gone?* www.preschoolerstoday.com/resources/articles/manners.htm